# Santa Fe

Meeting of the Chiefs *by Hernando Villa*
*BNSF Railway Art Collection*

# The Chief Way

**Robert Strein**
**John Vaughan**
**C. Fenton Richards Jr.**

1

*The 1951 Super Chief in an original lithograph used to promote the re-equipped train when new sleeping cars, dining cars and the famous Pleasure Dome lounge cars were introduced.*

# Acknowledgments

*A Santa Fe Railway postcard shows the Super Chief in Apache Canyon, N.M., circa 1956.*

The authors thank the following people and organizations for their assistance in the production of this book: Connie Menninger, Nancy Sherbert and the staff of the Kansas State Historical Society in Topeka for assisting us in our review of the Santa Fe Railway collection of photographs; Charles Larrabee, Albuquerque native and life-long Santa Fe Railway scholar, for reviewing the initial manuscript and for providing many suggestions and corrections to the final version of the text; Mo Palmer from the Albuquerque Museum Photo Archives for her help in locating the historic photographs of Hollywood celebrities passing through Albuquerque on the train; Jim Holbrook for his careful and expert photography of all of the Santa Fe Railway memorabilia seen in glorious color throughout the book; Ernest Robart, New Mexico native and photographer extraordinaire, for allowing us to review his extensive collection of Santa Fe Railway photographs and to use those selected for Chapter 8 of the book; and last, but not least, the Burlington Northern Santa Fe Railway Company for giving us permission to show all the Santa Fe Railway material in this book. Without the help of all of these individuals this book would never have gotten on track.

**Authors:** Robert Strein
John Vaughan
C. Fenton Richards Jr.

**Editor:** Arnold Vigil

**Copy Editor:** Ree Strange Sheck

**Book Design:** John Vaughan

**Production:** Linda J. Sanchez

**Publisher:** Ethel Hess

**Associate Publisher:** Jon Bowman

**Production Consultant:** Bette Brodsky

Library of Congress
Catalog Card Number: 2001-130302
ISBN: 0-937206-71-7

*Cover*—The Red Cliffs of Western New Mexico *by Adolph Heinze*
*Courtesy of the Burlington Northern and Santa Fe Railway Company*

# Dedications

*To Mom and Dad, who brought me to New Mexico in 1949 and took me on many unforgetable trips aboard Santa Fe's streamliners.*
**—Robert Strein**

*To the memory of my grandfather Papa John, who always rode the San Francisco Chief to New Mexico.*

*To the memory of Betsy Bryant Rose, who loved Santa Fe streamliners and the romance of the rails.*
**—John Vaughan**

This poster was used in ticket offices, depots and also was sold to individuals. The portrait of the Indian chief was used in other promotional items as well.

# Table of Contents

*The Super Chief speeds past the Devil's Footstool, a rock formation near Cerrillos, N.M., in the 1950s.*

# Foreword

By John Vaughan

*My sister, Janet Vaughan Schwandt, and I in front of the Big Dome lounge car on the San Francisco Chief in Clovis, N.M., circa 1955.*

*The San Francisco Chief glides into Clovis, N.M., from the east. I took this photograph with a Kodak Brownie Hawkeye camera in 1955.*

**S**ome of my fondest childhood memories are of my family's annual summer road trips from my hometown of Hobbs, N.M., to Clovis, N.M., to meet the westbound San Francisco Chief. My grandfather Papa John rode the train, traveling from Nebraska every summer to visit us.

We always arrived at the depot early, allowing me time to go to the ticket counter and drool over the huge rack of timetables beyond my reach. There were hundreds of them, it seemed, and they represented every passenger rail line in the country. They were bright and colorful with images of streamliners all over them. I fantasized about being allowed behind the counter where I could take one of each.

But I was too intimidated by the ticket agent to ask and I thought that a mere 10-year-old boy would be dismissed as being greedy or silly. Twenty years or so later, my fantasy came true when a wonderful ticket agent at the depot in El Paso, Texas, allowed me to go behind the counter and take as many timetables as I wanted. I will never forget his kindness and generosity.

Soon it was time to watch for the train. The distinct smell of creosote, which oozed from the wooden ties in the hot summer sun, was like an aphrodisiac to my senses. Heat waves rose from the ground and blurred the horizon as I peered down the endless track. Daddy urged me to place a penny on the iron rail and mark the spot so I could retrieve it after the train flattened it. Suddenly, a bright rotating light appeared through the swirling heat waves. It came closer and closer until the nose of the San Francisco Chief, which was painted like a red and yellow Indian warbonnet, came into full view.

I stood as close to the tracks as possible to feel the heat from the giant engines. The long string of stainless-steel cars glided to a smooth stop. Suddenly there was a flurry of activity as porters opened Dutch doors and placed step boxes for the passengers to detrain. A loudspeaker at a greasy spoon near the depot wailed in a Texas drawl, "Get your hot fried chicken—get it while it's nice and hot!" People immediately swarmed all over the brick platform. Soon we spotted Papa John in the crowd in his dapper suit and hat. People dressed up when they rode the train back in the 1950s.

I wanted to look inside the train. Daddy said I could walk through it but to make darn sure I was off of it before it started rolling to the west. I entered with mixed feelings of excitement and fear. I walked through each car and soaked up the ambiance. It was cool and there was a pleasing odor in the cars. I climbed the stairs to the Big Dome lounge under a panoramic glass. What a view! People in the sub-dome bar laughed and drank, while porters cleaned up and helped new passengers settle in.

I spotted a timetable someone left behind. Wow! I picked it up and still have it to this day. Suddenly, I heard, "All aboard!" I panicked, thinking I would end up in San Francisco. But I managed to get off right before the doors slammed shut. I stood by the elegant streamliner as it picked up speed—the stainless-steel cars soon became a glistening blur. I watched as it headed west in a cloud of dust, the red mars light on the rear car barely visible through the haze.

It was all over as soon as it began and an eerie silence befell the platform. My love for Santa Fe streamliners began right then and there and it's just as passionate today. I went back to the empty track and found my flattened penny and it remains a valued treasure in my collection of railroad memorabilia.

*The new San Francisco Chief is depicted in this stylized illustration used to advertise the 1954 streamliner—the last passenger train to be introduced by a railroad.*

# Introduction

*This Santa Fe brochure for the California Limited was issued in 1906. The cover illustration is one of the earliest known uses of Native Americans in Santa Fe advertising.*

The Atchison, Topeka and Santa Fe Railway became a part of the American Southwest in November 1878 when construction crews working from the east reached the summit of Ratón Pass and entered the Territory of New Mexico for the first time. Over the next several years the railroad extended its tracks south to Albuquerque and El Paso, and westward from Albuquerque to Arizona and California.

In the process of building through New Mexico, the Santa Fe encountered lofty mountain ranges, cut through spectacular canyons and skirted multicolored mesas and rock formations. It also passed by numerous Indian pueblos still inhabited as they had been for many hundreds of years. Next to its tracks towns sprang up and a new prosperity spread through the territory. From its earliest beginnings the Santa Fe Railway profoundly impacted New Mexico and the Southwest. But soon the American Southwest and its Native American people profoundly influenced the railway.

This influence manifested in many ways, from the names the railroad gave its passenger trains and cars to decoration, both inside and out. Indian symbols even adorned the china used in the dining cars. For many years Indians from several Southwestern tribes actually rode the trains through New Mexico, acting as guides for fascinated passengers. The Southwest's influence is most apparent in the railroad's advertising. Beginning as early as the 1880s, images of Southwestern landscapes and Native people were used in promotional material, and these images became more and more widespread as time went by. By the late 1940s and 1950s this advertising campaign had developed into a virtual artform.

No other railroad, and perhaps no other company in the history of America, so completely embraced the territory it served and used the mystique of a land and its people to market itself to its customers. As a result, the Santa Fe Railway's image of sleek, streamlined passenger trains crossing New Mexico became known throughout the country, and people flocked to Santa Fe trains to see the Southwest for themselves.

This book conveys the excitement and romance of streamlined train travel on the Santa Fe and provides a look at how the railroad used the landscapes and Indian culture of the American Southwest to promote travel on its famous trains.

*The first use of the little Indian boy, Chico, is seen in this early ad promoting "Santa Fe All the Way." This same illustration was used on timetables and posters in the late 1940s and '50s.*

*Above*—Passenger timetable dated January 26, 1947.

*Right*—The cover of a California Limited brochure issued in December 1927.

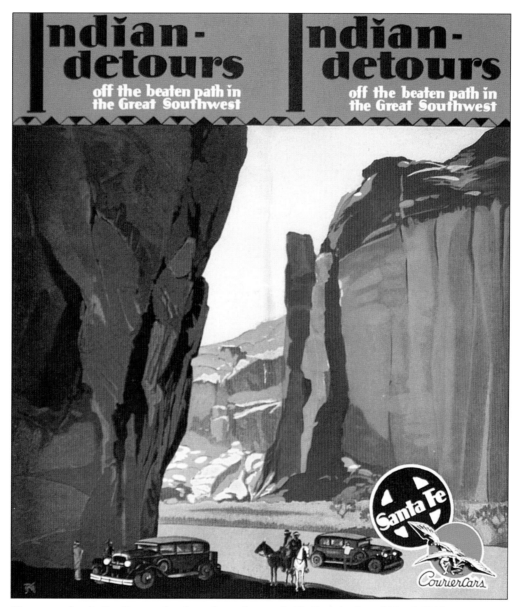

*The cover of an Indian Detours brochure shows Canyon de Chelly, Ariz., issued March 1938.*

# The Chiefs

*One of the first brochures for the new Santa Fe Chief issued in February 1927. This brochure shows an early use of color in the Indian motif.*

In November 1926, the Santa Fe Railway placed into service a new first-class, all-Pullman sleeping-car train that ran daily between Chicago and Los Angeles. They named the train the Chief, a name that would become known from coast to coast. The Santa Fe previously operated luxury passenger trains, namely the California Limited and the de Luxe, but the Chief raised the standard for fast luxury service. The train was touted as "Extra Fast, Extra Fine, Extra Fare" and covered the miles between Chicago and Los Angeles in a then-unprecedented time of 63 hours, quite an accomplishment for a heavyweight train pulled by steam locomotives. The train carried Pullman sleeping cars with a variety of accommodations, a club car, dining car and an observation sun-parlor car. The Chief offered such refinements as a ladies' lounge and maid, barber, valet and manicure service as well as shower baths. A 1927 brochure described the Chief as follows:

*As a befitting conveyance to and from the new America and the old, the Santa Fe Railway has installed the Chief, the most commodious and luxurious train on rails. The Chief has garnered in its appointments and conveniences all the luxuries that lie between the Atlantic and Pacific. The refinements of the finest hotels, clubs, and restaurants are found in this magnificent palace on wheels. The charm of the East and the West meet and commingle in surroundings that administer minutely to the most fastidious tastes.*

For the next 10 years the Chief remained the pride of the railroad and continued to receive new equipment as it was ordered. However, in the mid-1930s the streamline era dawned for American railroads and the Santa Fe was not to be left behind. The railroad began working with General Motors and the Budd Co. of Philadelphia on the design of a brand new, high-speed luxury train. The result was the new streamlined Super Chief, the first diesel-powered, all-Pullman sleeping-car train in America, and it eclipsed the Chief as Santa Fe's standard-bearer.

The new Super Chief made its maiden run from Dearborn Station in Chicago on May 18, 1937, and covered the 2,222 miles to Los Angeles in just 39 hours and 45 minutes. With only one set of equipment the train operated but once a week from both Chicago and Los Angeles. From that day the Super Chief set the standard for luxury rail travel in America.

Following the introduction of the tremendously popular Super Chief, the Santa Fe received enough new light-weight, streamlined passenger cars in 1938 to equip 13 additional trains. This included enough equipment to replace the six Chief heavyweight consists and to add a second Super Chief to the Chicago-Los Angeles run. Two new sets of equipment were also used to usher in a completely new concept in modern train travel. These new trains were each named El Capitan and provided economy-minded coach travelers with a level of service never before seen in America. These trains operated twice a week between Chicago and Los Angeles and provided modern, deluxe coach, lounge and dining-car service at speeds equal to the famed Super Chief.

Santa Fe passenger service was stretched to the limit during World War II because of the unprecedented demands of wartime travel. After the war the Santa Fe immediately began ordering new streamlined passenger cars to replace aging equipment. Enough new cars were received by 1948 to completely re-equip the Super Chief and El Capitan and

*The Chief rounds a curve in Arizona around 1956. Note the Big Dome lounge car near the center of the train. Courtesy of the Kansas State Historical Society.*

*The eastbound Chief descends Ratón Pass in Colorado around 1956. Passengers watched the passing scenery in luxurious comfort aboard the Big Dome lounge car seen in the foreground. Courtesy of the Kansas State Historical Society.*

to begin running both trains on a daily basis. Another new train also was inaugurated—the streamlined Texas Chief, operating between Chicago and Houston/Galveston. In 1950, another new streamliner was created, the Kansas City Chief, operating overnight between Chicago and Kansas City.

With all of this new equipment, Santa Fe's passenger service was certainly first-rate, but the railroad continued to provide its passengers with the best service possible. In January 1951, the Super Chief was again re-equipped with new sleeping cars, dining cars and the first dome lounge cars built for the Santa Fe. These dome lounge cars were called Pleasure Dome cars and they truly were luxurious. The forward section of each car contained a spacious lounge area with sofas, chairs, tables and a writing desk stocked with distinctive Super Chief stationery. Upstairs, the glass-enclosed dome section contained individual swivel lounge chairs for viewing the passing scenery. Under the dome was a cozy cocktail lounge staffed by an expert Santa Fe bartender and at the rear of the car was the first private dining room aboard any train in the country. This room was named the Turquoise Room and seated 12 people for private luncheon, cocktail or dinner parties. The re-equipping of the Super Chief also included new dining cars that seated 36 patrons in a very plush environment while serving quality Fred Harvey cuisine. The Fred Harvey Co. had operated the dining-car service on all Santa Fe trains since 1888.

In 1954, the railroad received 14 full-length dome lounge cars for service on El Capitan trains. The dome sections of these cars were much larger than those of the Pleasure Dome cars and, in fact, could seat 75 passengers. Six of these new dome lounges also were added to another new Santa Fe train, the San Francisco Chief, placed into service in June 1954 between Chicago and the San Francisco Bay area. This train was the last new transcontinental passenger train to be placed into service in America and became extremely popular.

Santa Fe continued its never-ending effort to provide the very best in rail-passenger equipment. In July 1956, the Santa Fe introduced its new Hi-Level El Capitan trains. These trains were unlike any others in the world. Each train consisted of double-deck coach cars, a dining car and lounge car. All seating was on the upper level for better viewing of the passing scenery and provided a quieter, smoother ride. Restroom facilities and luggage storage were on the lower levels of the coaches. The Hi-Level dining cars could seat 80 patrons at a time on the upper level. The kitchen was on the lower level and the food was delivered to the upper level on a small elevator. Lounge cars had windows extending over the roof for better viewing of the passing countryside and a large lounge area on the upper level with tables, chairs, bar and a newsstand. The downstairs section of these cars contained a coffee shop, providing light meals and refreshments. These new trains offered the ultimate in comfortable, economy coach travel. Additional Hi-Level cars were received as late as 1964, also allowing Hi-Level coaches to be placed on the San Francisco Chief.

Throughout its history the Santa Fe Railway was known for the quality of its passenger-train service. The absolute ultimate in luxurious, fast and comfortable train travel occurred during the streamline era from 1937 until 1971, when the Santa Fe (and most other railroads) turned over its passenger service to Amtrak.

*This beautiful illustration appeared in a 1927 Chief brochure. Note the stylized Chief emblem on the drumhead.*

*Be carefree, be comfortable and enjoy a*

# New World Standard in Travel

## The new Santa Fe

# Super Chief

**Advanced ideas for your travel luxury…new cradled smoothness in the ride…daily between Los Angeles and Chicago**

From the flanges on the wheels to the tip of the restful Pleasure Dome, the Super Chief is new—entirely new.

To give you the smoothest ride of your life on rails, this new Super Chief glides on cushioned springs…revises any ideas you ever had about any train.

The keynote is comfort.

You find it in the distinctive Turquoise Room in the lounge car—a delightful place to relax, enjoy a cocktail or entertain your friends at dinner—the first time such a room has been provided on any train.

You find it in the Pleasure Dome—"top of the

Super, next to the stars"—that brings you an unobstructed view of southwestern scenery.

You find it in the new dining cars where Fred Harvey chefs present new and exciting menus.

Accommodations in this beautiful all-room train pamper you every mile of the way… "push-button" radio or music in your room when you *want* it…beds you just can't help sleeping in …charming apartments by day.

For your next trip between Los Angeles and Chicago say "Super Chief." Now, more than ever, it is America's train of trains. Just consult your local ticket or travel agent.

**SANTA FE SYSTEM LINES**
*Serving the West and Southwest*

Santa Fe

*This two-page advertisement was introduced to promote the new, re-equipped 1951 Super Chief. Notice the similarity of the illustration seen in the lithograph on Page 2. Most major magazines such as* Life, Time, *and* The Saturday Evening Post *ran this ad during the introductory period.*

*The Pleasure Dome lounge car is seen here on the westbound Super Chief as it ascends Ratón Pass in Colorado. The Pleasure Dome lounge contained swivel chairs in the dome, a spacious main lounge, a cozy sub-dome cocktail lounge and bar, and the first private dining room on rails— the Turquoise Room. Courtesy of the Kansas State Historical Society.*

*Above*—A late 1930s postcard features the new streamlined Super Chief introduced in 1937.

*Right*—An illustration from a 1937 Super Chief brochure.

*The cover of a 1937 Super Chief brochure.*

*A brand new Pleasure Dome lounge car built for the 1951 Super Chief sits on display in San Diego, Calif., before being placed into revenue service. The dome lounges and new dining cars were displayed in numerous cities around the rail system.*

*The cover of a late 1940s brochure for the Super Chief displays the drumhead used for many years.*

*The 1951 Super Chief was the best the Santa Fe had to offer. The brochure above was printed on heavy stock and contained illustrations of most of the car interiors.*

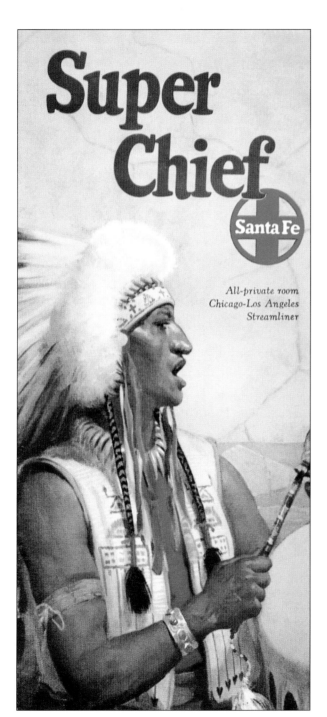

*A 1951 Super Chief rounds a curve at Ratón Pass on this postcard produced by the Santa Fe Railway.*

*All of the dining and lounge cars on the Super Chief were refurbished and redecorated in 1958. The 11-double-bedroom sleeping car was introduced. This brochure displayed the new interiors.*

*A Santa Fe Railway promotional photograph of a new 1951 Super Chief on the horseshoe curve in Ribera, N.M. Courtesy of the Kansas State Historical Society.*

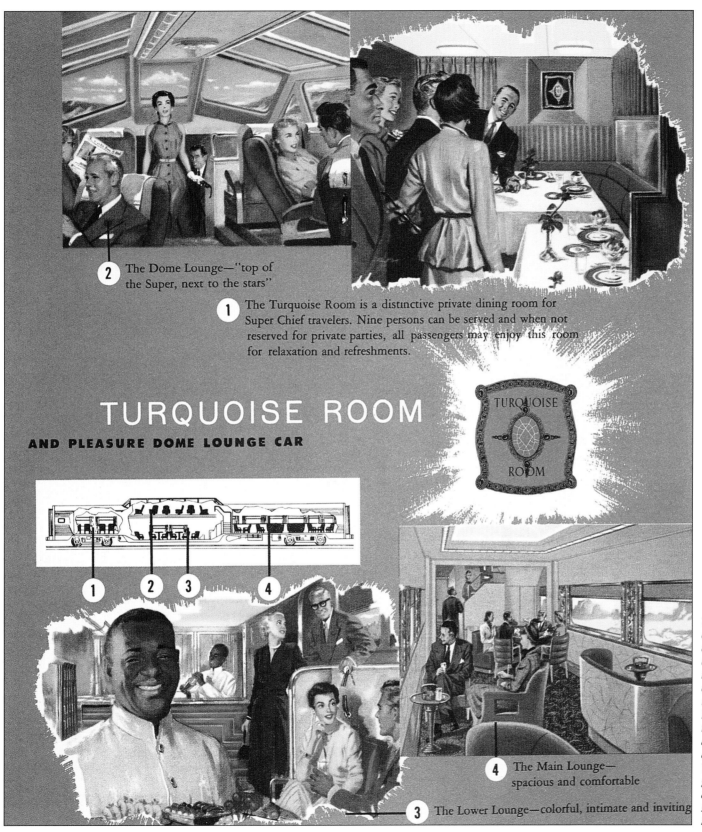

**2** The Dome Lounge—"top of the Super, next to the stars"

**1** The Turquoise Room is a distinctive private dining room for Super Chief travelers. Nine persons can be served and when not reserved for private parties, all passengers may enjoy this room for relaxation and refreshments.

# TURQUOISE ROOM
## AND PLEASURE DOME LOUNGE CAR

TURQUOISE ROOM

**1** **2** **3** **4**

**4** The Main Lounge— spacious and comfortable

**3** The Lower Lounge—colorful, intimate and inviting

*The Pleasure Dome lounge car on the 1951 Super Chief was one of the most luxurious cars ever made for any train. The most famous inovation in this car was the first private dining room on rails, the Turquoise Room. It could be reserved anytime, day or night, for private dinner parties, cocktail parties or any other special event. When not in use, other passengers could enjoy the ambiance of this special room. This spread is from an early 1950s Super Chief brochure.*

All-Chair-Car Transcontinental Streamliner
via the Route of the Super Chief and The Chief

**Above**—*The cover of a 1948 brochure for the all-coach El Capitan.*

**Right**—*In 1954, El Capitan trains received new chair cars and the majestic Big Dome lounge cars. A new brochure was produced to highlight this new equipment.*

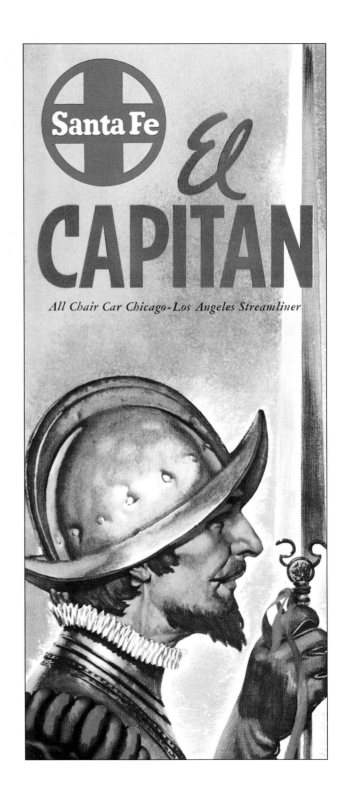

Santa Fe *El* CAPITAN

*All Chair Car Chicago-Los Angeles Streamliner*

# New "BIG DOME" LOUNGE CAR

**Fun in the "BIG DOME"**

The scenic upper level of the "Big Dome" is delightful for a panoramic view of passing towns and scenes along the route of El Capitan. Refreshments are available in the "Big Dome" lounge section during the day and early evening hours.

## TOPS IN FUN
## TOPS IN TRAVEL

Designed for pleasure from end to end, from top to bottom, the "Big Dome" Lounge Car has 57 sofa seats— each angled to give passengers a full window view, and a refreshment lounge for 18 on the scenic upper level. On the lower level is a colorful cocktail lounge for 28 persons.

This new "Big Dome" lounge adds more fun, more interest and makes it easier for you to see the colorful route El Capitan travels through the scenic Southwest.

*All cars on El Capitan are equipped to provide music, radio and train announcements to make your trip more interesting.*

**Fun in the Lower Lounge**

In complete contrast with the spacious "Big Dome" is the intimate, colorful lower lounge seating 28 passengers.

**Now an Indian Guide on El Capitan**

A real Indian in full tribal costume now rides El Capitan (westbound) across New Mexico to tell you about the scenery, history and legends of the land you see through the train window.

*In 1954, Santa Fe purchased Big Dome lounge cars for El Capitan and San Francisco Chief trains. These magnificent cars rode on six-wheel trucks and were the heaviest cars at that time. The entire upper level provided luxurious seating for viewing the scenery. Curved sofas with tables were also available on the upper level. Nestled beneath the dome was an intimate lounge and bar decorated with illuminated glass panels featuring Hopi kachina figures.*

**Above**—*Passenger timetable dated June 8, 1969.*

**Right**—*This impressive, colorful two-page advertisement was for the new Hi-Level El Capitan and appeared in several magazines such as* Holiday, Life *and* The Saturday Evening Post.

# Step aboard th

### Let us show you around tl

You can see at a glance it's different, because it's so tall and sleek, but you won't realize how different—how quiet and smooth—until you actually ride it. So step aboard this new kind of all-coach train, and let us show you around.

# new Hi-level train

## igher, quieter, smoother El Capitan

**Ever see such roomy baggage racks?** The porter keeps your baggage here, on the lower level of your car, out of your way. And isn't it nice to be able to travel with *all* the luggage you need?

**There's always a "show" going on.** It's right outside your window. And when you go Hi-Level, you're up where you can see it all . . . as you relax in your stretch-out sleeper seat.

**A picture window 2,224 miles long.** No place like this dome lounge to see the sights—or just to relax over cool refreshments, conversation or a hand of gin rummy.

**Coffee-break in the Kachina Lounge.** Make yourself comfortable in the quiet, intimate Kachina coffee shop in the lower lounge for a quick snack. Service from dawn to midnight.

**You dine Hi-Level, too.** Feast your eyes on the scenery—and yourself on the famous Fred Harvey budget meals. With soft music and impeccable

# $66 12

(plus tax)
one way between
Chicago-Los Angeles,
including extra fare.
Lower with Family Fares.

*For reservations, consult
the nearest railroad or travel agent.*

## *New* HI-LEVEL El Capitan

## TIME TABLE

**1968 ★★★ 2068**

Santa Fe

OUR SECOND CENTURY OF PROGRESS

**The Atchison, Topeka and Santa Fe Railway Co.**

*Condensed
Schedules of
Passenger Service*

*Issued:
July 15, 1968*

*Passenger timetable dated July 15, 1968.*

*The all-coach El Capitan was completely transformed into a two-story train with the introduction of the Hi-Level cars in 1956. These Hi-Level cars were quieter and smoother than their predecessors and won instant popularity with the passengers. Here, the train descends Glorieta Pass in New Mexico. Courtesy of the Kansas State Historical Society.*

*Cover of the brochure for the Hi-Level El Capitan, circa 1958.*

*Apache Canyon in New Mexico is the setting for this postcard showing the new Hi-Level El Capitan of 1956.*

*The Hi-Level El Capitan speeds through New Mexico's Shoemaker Canyon.*

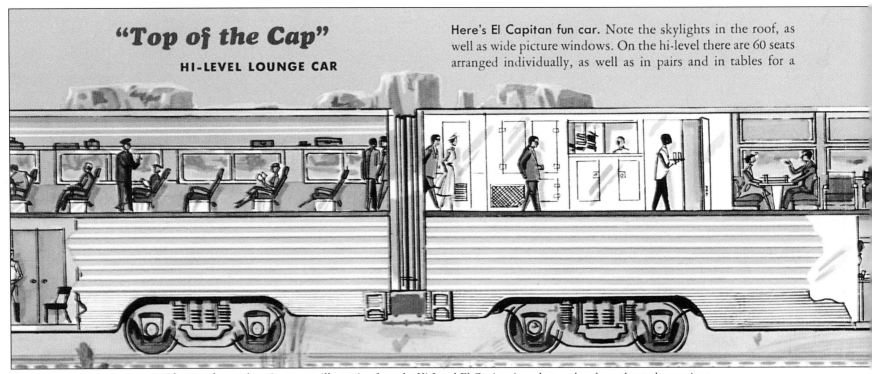

**"Top of the Cap"**

HI-LEVEL LOUNGE CAR

Here's El Capitan fun car. Note the skylights in the roof, as well as wide picture windows. On the hi-level there are 60 seats arranged individually, as well as in pairs and in tables for a

*Above and opposite*—A cutaway illustration from the Hi-Level El Capitan introductory brochure shows the spacious lounge car.

*The cover of the introductory brochure for the new Hi-Level El Capitan, June 1956.*

foursome of bridge. The stairway at center of car leads to the lower lounge accommodating 20 more passengers. There is a refreshment bar and attendants on both levels, also on the upper level is a completely stocked newsstand. There is plenty of room to move around in this new type lounge car and in all the other cars that make up the Hi-Level El Capitan. This roominess is just one of many features that contribute to the smooth-riding comfort of El Capitan.

*This Santa Fe Railway postcard shows the Hi-Level lounge car on El Capitan.*

The coach seats in the Hi-Level El Capitan were the most comfortable available at that time. Leg rests could be raised or lowered and legroom was very generous.

**Below and opposite**—A cutaway view of the Hi-Level diner on El Capitan. The diner was the largest and the heaviest ever used on a streamlined passenger train and thus rode on six-wheel trucks.

*A panel from the Hi-Level El Capitan introductory brochure depicts the wonderful dining and lounge cars. The diner kitchen was on the lower level and food was transported to the upper level via dumbwaiter.*

above the noise of the kitchen below. 80 passengers can be served at one sitting in this spacious dining car and everyone is pleased with the economically priced meals.

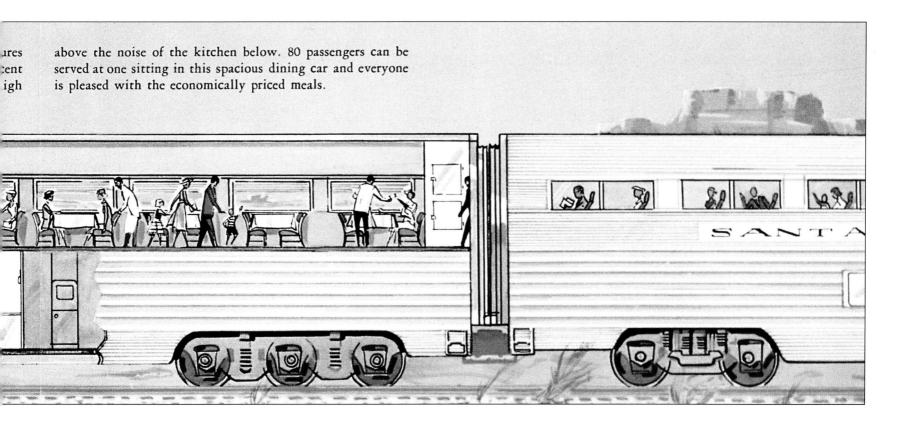

*A lengthy San Francisco Chief climbs the grade in Abó Canyon east of Belén, N.M. Hi-Level chair cars had been added to this train in the 1960s and can be seen at the center of the consist. Courtesy of the Kansas State Historical Society.*

*The cover of a San Francisco Chief brochure, April 1957.*

*The cover of a Texas Chief brochure, April 1957.*

# "Let's take the train!"

*This promotional brochure printed in the mid-1960s covered the major streamliners then in operation. Interior pictures and brief descriptions of each train were included in this piece.*

**E**ven before the Santa Fe Railway reached the Territory of New Mexico it promoted travel on its trains. Referring to itself as the "land hunters, gold hunters, and buffalo hunters road," the railway targeted farmers, ranchers and miners in its early advertising. Settlers were encouraged to buy land from the railroad in western Kansas and eastern Colorado, then travel to their newly acquired land on the Santa Fe. They also informed miners that the Santa Fe was the easiest way to reach the gold and silver fields of the Colorado Rockies.

By the late 1800s, however, providing transportation to settlers and miners proved less lucrative as tourism and leisure travel became more popular. Train travel also became more comfortable with the addition of private-room sleeping cars, dining cars and lounge cars on long-distance trains. Santa Fe advertising now began to describe the advantages of train travel—the comfort, the speed, the safety. Accompanied by intricate black-and-white sketches, Santa Fe promotional material at the turn of the century went to great lengths to describe the many accommodations and amenities available to passengers on its trains. These descriptions often bordered on the fanciful. Take for example the following from a 1906 brochure for the California Limited:

> *Ahead may be heard the impatient engine, anxious to begin its relay contest with prairie winds and mountain grades. This luxurious train is certainly inviting—so warm, so full of light and color! It is to be a home on wheels for many travelers during the next three days en route to the land where every month is June. Congenial persons—educated, refined and well dressed—are the kind one meets here, because this is the only train between Chicago and Southern California, via any line, exclusively for first-class travel. The journey is sure to be pleasant socially.*

When the Santa Fe inaugurated the Chief in 1926, brochures continued to describe the luxurious accommodations and amenities on board the train, but now these brochures contained color illustrations. Travel time also became more important and advertising emphasized that the Chief was the fastest train between Chicago and southern California. The standard raised even higher with the introduction of the streamlined Super Chief in 1937. For the first time, black-and-white photographs were used as advertising became more refined.

Advertising to encourage travel was curtailed during World War II as all efforts were placed on providing essential military transportation. With the end of the war and the lifting of travel restrictions, however, Americans eagerly started traveling again and the Santa Fe anxiously attracted as many of these travelers as possible. Hundreds of new streamlined passenger cars were received by 1948, and the Santa Fe embarked on an intensive advertising campaign to attract passengers to its new trains. In addition to railroad-produced brochures, the Santa Fe ran full-page ads, many in color, in such popular magazines as *Life, Holiday, The Saturday Evening Post* and *National Geographic.* This sophisticated advertising campaign continued well into the early 1960s.

Ads for the Super Chief targeted the first-class traveler and showed refined and well-dressed passengers enjoying their private accommodations or dining on gourmet meals in the Fred Harvey dining car, while being doted upon by the steward and attentive waiters. Passengers were also shown in the Pleasure Dome lounge car absorbing the passing scenery from the dome or enjoying a cocktail in the downstairs lounge.

*This photograph appeared in a circa-1940 brochure for both the Super Chief and the Chief. Passengers are boarding the California-bound Chief at Dearborn Station in Chicago.*

*Passengers enjoy the ambiance of the lower cocktail lounge in one of the Big Dome lounge cars. Notice the etched glass panels with Hopi kachina figures. These were illuminated at night. Indian designs also graced the Formica tabletops. Courtesy of the Kansas State Historical Society.*

*Far left*—A full-page ad for all three of the major Santa Fe trains in the mid-1950s. The famous Turquoise Room of the Super Chief is shown at the top.

*Left*—A full-page advertisement for the spectacular Big Dome lounge cars introduced in 1954.

The most intriguing ads showed diners comfortably settled into the cozy tables of the Turquoise Room. One of the more famous ads for the Super Chief depicted an elegant young woman (no doubt a movie star) walking down a station platform past the observation lounge car of the Super Chief while being photographed by the press. "She came in on the Super Chief. How else would she travel to and from California?" stated the caption on the ad.

But the railroad advertised other things besides its top-notch Super Chief. Ads also were produced for economy-minded travelers likely to be attracted to El Capitan and other Santa Fe trains. Passengers in these ads were shown enjoying the spaciousness of their reclining-seat coaches or the amenities available to them in the lounges and dining cars. Many ads also showed Santa Fe's courier nurses offering assistance to young and old travelers.

Other ads depicted scenic Southwestern locations of interest to tourists rather than the actual trains. These ads included such famous sights as Grand Canyon, Monument Valley, Carlsbad Caverns and Rainbow Bridge, and they primarily appeared in *National Geographic* magazine.

By the 1960s ads became more simple and illustrative, but the Santa Fe continued to promote its passenger service even when automobiles and airlines severely impacted train travel. Long after many other railroads all but gave up on their passenger trains, the Santa Fe continued to operate a quality service and still advertised to attract customers to its trains.

*This full-page ad for the Super Chief says it all. Luxurious surroundings and outstanding food were the hallmarks of this famous streamliner.*

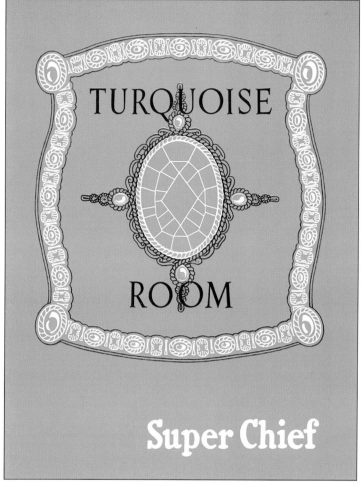

*Above*—The large embossed menu cover used exclusively in the Turquoise Room was made to hold the regular-size menu inside.

*Left*—A romantic photograph of a couple in the Turquoise Room highlights this evocative ad from the early 1960s.

*Above*—The main lounge of the Pleasure Dome car on the Super Chief after it was refurbished and redecorated in 1958. Behind the ornamental screen is a writing desk with embossed Super Chief stationary. Courtesy of the Kansas State Historical Society.

*Right*—The Super Chief always had a reputation for luxury and elegant service. As a result, many Hollywood celebrities rode the train between Chicago and Los Angeles. This ad was produced to appeal to an upscale clientele.

*The Pleasure Dome on the Super Chief was a most popular spot and was almost always full. It was one of the few domes that had rotating easy chairs for maximum viewing.*

"Turquoise Room," Santa Fe Super Chief

# Smartest place to eat between Chicago and Los Angeles

For its size, this is the most famous restaurant in all the world. It's the Turquoise Room on the *Super Chief*.

Transcontinental commuters, of whom the Santa Fe has quite a number, love the feeling of a private club enroute that the Turquoise Room gives them.

For example, one of our recent passengers happened to have a birthday aboard, and his wife engaged the room for a surprise party (you can do that). Where else but on the Santa Fe would you find such unexpected extra services?

It's America's new railroad, and new things are coming fast. If you haven't traveled with us recently, you have some pleasant surprises in store. Enjoy them soon, won't you?

*The Super Chief*—*all-room streamlined train daily between Chicago and Los Angeles.*
**Also daily:** *The Chief and El Capitan (between Chicago and Los Angeles) . . . San Francisco Chief (between Chicago and San Francisco).*

Santa Fe

*The elegant Turquoise Room on the Super Chief featured its own china, which has since become extremely rare and sought after by collectors.*

**44**

Find out **how fine** a train can be

Perhaps it's the thoughtful service. Or the Fred Harvey food. Or... as seasoned travelers put it, there's just nothing like the Super Chief. Won't you join us?

**EXTRA FARE—AND WORTH IT!**

Santa Fe

**Super Chief**

**Above**—The couple shown in this Santa Fe promotional photograph are enjoying the famous Super Chief "Champagne Dinner." Beautiful Mimbreño china and heavy cutlery were always used in the dining car of the Super Chief. The food was the best on rails. Courtesy of the Kansas State Historical Society.

**Left**—Holiday Magazine ran many ads for the Super Chief in the 1960s, such as this one featuring the Turquoise Room.

*Above*—A couple relaxes in the reclining chairs of the new Hi-Level El Capitan. Compare the space and legroom with today's cramped airline seating. Courtesy of the Kansas State Historical Society.

*Right*—This illustration of El Capitan arriving at the Albuquerque station was used on the cover of the route brochure "Along the Way" in the 1950s. The beautiful Alvarado Hotel to the left was demolished in 1970.

El Capitan arriving Albuquerque

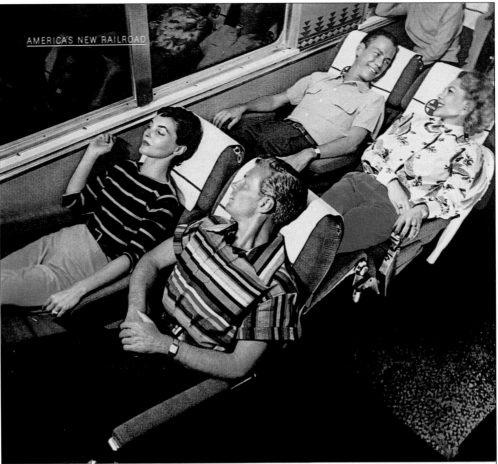

America's New Railroad

*On Santa Fe's famous streamliners—El Capitan, The Chief, San Francisco Chief*

## Even the cost is comfortable—only $55.44 PLUS TAX

### All the way—either way—between Chicago and California

You'll have fun, too!

You'll stroll around and get acquainted with interesting people aboard . . . sip a refreshing drink in the lounge car . . . taste those marvelous Fred Harvey meals . . . see the colorful Southwest Indian Country from different parts of the train.

And back in your reclining chair, you press the button or lift the leg rest and your chair fits you . . . and your mood, too. It's easily adjusted to more than 100 comfortable ways.

You can sit up and enjoy the scenery. Or you can stretch out your legs, lean back, and let that drowsy nod become a refreshing nap.

So reserve one of the new "stretchout" chairs on *El Capitan* or *The Chief* (Chicago-Los Angeles) or the *San Francisco Chief* (Chicago-San Francisco).

Remember, it costs only $55.44 one way (round trip just $90.15) plus tax.

Santa Fe

WHEN YOU GET THERE . . . RENT A CAR

*Economy-chair car travel was never more luxurious than it was on El Capitan. There was more room and comfort than most first-class seating on today's airlines.*

*The Big Dome lounge cars offered seating for viewing and intimate lounge seating for a game of cards, a cocktail or a lively conversation with fellow passengers. One of Santa Fe's courier nurses visits with passengers aboard this streamliner. Courtesy of the Kansas State Historical Society.*

*The intimate cocktail lounge in the Pleasure Dome car on the Super Chief was very popular with passengers. This Santa Fe promotional photograph shows the interior as it looked after being redecorated in 1958. Complimentary hors d'oeuvres were served during the cocktail hour. Navajo sand paintings were installed on the front of the bar in each car. Courtesy of the Kansas State Historical Society.*

*This ad appeared in* National Geographic *in 1951 to announce the new Super Chief when it was completely re-equipped with new cars.*

*Above*—This colorful beverage menu was used for many years on Santa Fe streamliners.

*Right*—This ad from the 1950s was used to promote the new Big Dome lounge cars introduced on El Capitan and San Francisco Chief in 1954.

*The Hi-Level diners on El Capitan were truly magnificent cars. They could seat up to 80 people at one sitting, and the food was prepared in the kitchen under the dining area and brought up via dumbwaiter to be served piping hot. Indian decor appeared throughout the car as seen in this promotional Santa Fe photograph. Courtesy of the Kansas State Historical Society.*

*A rare full-page ad produced in the late 1940s shows one of the beautiful Alco PA locomotives used on some of the Santa Fe streamliners.*

The Alvarado Hotel... ALBUQUERQUE, NEW MEXICO
Fred Harvey "3000 MILES OF HOSPITALITY" Series
See back of menu for description and further details about this series.

*Above*—The menu cover used by Fred Harvey for the Alvarado Hotel in Albuquerque, N.M.

*Right*—Today, La Fonda Hotel in Santa Fe, N.M., remains much as it was in the 1940s and '50s. It was the departure point for the famous Indian Detours operated by Fred Harvey in the 1930s and '40s. Both menus date to circa 1955.

La Fonda Hotel... SANTA FE, NEW MEXICO
Fred Harvey "3000 MILES OF HOSPITALITY" Series
See back of menu for description and further details about this series.

*For many years, the Santa Fe employed courier nurses on many of its trains. All of these young women were registered nurses and assisted passengers in any way they could. They were especially helpful to mothers traveling with small children and to elderly passengers. They served as a source for information of all kinds and were available all hours of the day or night. In this promotional photograph, we see a courier nurse sporting the summer uniform used in the 1960s. This photograph was taken in the upper-level lounge of the Hi-Level El Capitan. Courtesy of the Kansas State Historical Society.*

*This ad from* National Geographic *depicts Rainbow Bridge in the Santa Fe Southwest.*

Everyone enjoys a big view from every seat of the Big Dome Car. On the lower level of these cars is an attendant and a refreshment lounge.

# Find out what fun a Santa Fe trip can be!

The unique Turquoise Room is a symbol of Super Chief finery. This intimate dining room is one of the many features of this famous streamliner. Highlight of the gourmet menu is the champagne dinner.

*This panel from a general brochure released in the early 1960s shows the interior of the Big Dome lounge car and the elegant Turquoise Room on the Super Chief.*

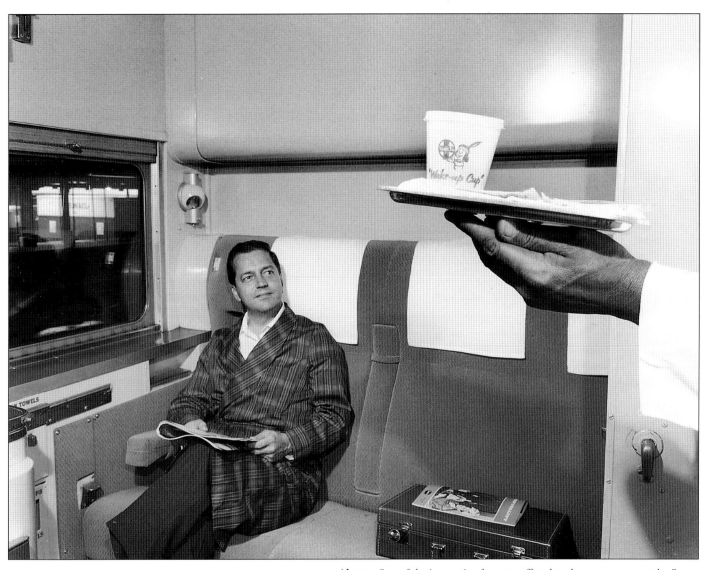

*Above*—One of the innovative features offered to the passengers on the Super Chief was the "Wake-Up Cup" of coffee. This service was brought right to your private bedroom. It was a great way to start the day. Courtesy of the Kansas State Historical Society.

*The main lounge of the Pleasure Dome lounge car on the Super Chief offered comfortable couches and tables for conversation, cards or a cocktail from the bar. Lounge areas on the Super Chief were at a premium, and the 1951 version offered two lounge cars and an observation lounge to the rear of the train. Courtesy of the Kansas State Historical Society.*

*Passenger timetable dated July 1, 1970.*

*A ticket envelope from the 1960s.*

*The service offered on the Super Chief was impeccable. Friendly porters were available day and night for just about anything you might want. Meal service was available to your private room, and many patrons took advantage of this amenity. Many of the porters worked the Super Chief their entire careers, and they knew many of the frequent passengers by name. Courtesy of the Kansas State Historical Society.*

## She came in on the *Super Chief*

How else would she travel to and from California?
For the Super Chief is one of the most glamorous all-private-room
trains in America, filled with people who know how to travel
and appreciate the best in travel.
It serves those famous Fred Harvey meals.
It operates on a 39¾-hour schedule between Chicago and Los Angeles.
The Super Chief (now in daily service) is the flag-bearer of
Santa Fe's fine fleet of Chicago-California trains.

**Santa Fe**

**SANTA FE SYSTEM LINES .. Serving the West and Southwest**

T. B. Gallaher, General Passenger Traffic Manager, Chicago 4

*The Super Chief was known as the "Train of the Stars." The Hollywood set used the "Super" (as it was affectionately known) to commute between California and the East. Scenes like the one depicted in this* National Geographic *ad often became reality as a star detrained in Los Angeles or Chicago.*

*The elegant round-end observation cars used on the Super Chief were wonderful examples of Art-Deco Modernism. This is one of the Vista-series cars used from the late 1940s to mid-'50s. It offered bedrooms and drawing rooms. A cozy lounge with easy chairs and sofas was located to the rear of the car. Courtesy of the Kansas State Historical Society.*

# The Land of Pueblos

FEBRUARY 29, 1948

**Santa Fe**

SANTA FE ALL THE WAY

**TIME TABLES**

The Atchison, Topeka and Santa Fe Railway System

*The most lasting and identifiable image used by the Santa Fe Railway was Chico. Here he graces the cover of a timetable from 1948.*

The earliest known use of a Native American image in Santa Fe advertising is an 1878 ad that targeted settlers and depicted an Indian chief telling "all braves that the happiest hunting grounds can be reached directly by the Santa Fe Railway." Throughout the next century images of Indians and exotic Southwestern landscapes became more and more prominent in Santa Fe advertising. These images were used in railroad-produced literature as well as in magazine and newspaper advertisements.

But the territory it served had other influences on the railroad besides advertising. Entire trains were named after Indian tribes such as the Hopi and the Navajo. The first Santa Fe Chief was inaugurated in 1926 and went on to spawn an entire tribe of famous Santa Fe trains that carried the Chief name. The first streamlined Super Chief was deliberately designed from head to tail to reflect the Southwest Indian culture. The red-and-silver diesel locomotives that pulled the trains displayed a paint scheme modeled after an Indian headdress (or warbonnet), and all of the stainless-steel passenger cars were named after Indian pueblos and tribes along the route of the train—Isleta, Laguna, Acoma, Cochití, Oraibi, Taos and Navajo. The car interiors, especially the lounge and dining cars, were decorated with Indian motifs and colors of the Southwest. Even the china used in the Fred Harvey dining car was unique. Each piece carried a reproduction of an ancient Indian design taken from historic pottery pieces made by the Mimbres Indians of southern New Mexico.

The large order of new streamlined cars received by the railroad in 1938 included 57 Pullman sleeping cars all bearing Native American names. Many people thought these names were made up because they were so seemingly unpronounceable, but all were named for actual places on the Indian reservations of New Mexico and Arizona. Some of the more intriguing names used were Tesuque, Moencopi, Kietsiel, Tchirege, Tsankawi, Toadlena, Betahtakin and Denehotso. All of these cars were used in first-class service on the Super Chief and Chief. What fun it is to imagine a family from Cleveland on their first trip west in 1940 as they walked down the station platform, trying to pronounce the names of cars before they boarded the Santa Fe Super Chief at Dearborn Station in Chicago. Then they discover their compartment is in a car named Toroweap! They probably felt like they entered some strange and faraway land before they even left Chicago. There is no doubt the Santa Fe chose these names for exactly that affect. Another order of new streamlined sleeping cars in 1947 continued the tradition of naming cars with Indian monikers. These cars, however, carried names such as Indian Arrow, Indian Drum, Indian Pony and Indian Scout, all much more pronounceable than the names of the 1938 cars.

After World War II, the railroad continued to build new streamlined cars with Indian-inspired interiors. Coaches had large silver medallions with Native American designs attached to interior walls. The Pleasure Dome lounge cars built for the Super Chief boasted elaborate Navajo sand paintings on the walls of the lounge section. The Big Dome lounge cars delivered in 1954 had interiors painted in Southwestern colors of turquoise, beige and rust. In the downstairs lounge below the dome, beautiful etched-glass partitions depicted Hopi kachinas that were illuminated at night.

But perhaps the most splendid cars of all were the Hi-Level cars built in 1956 for El Capitan. The interiors of all these cars were painted in Southwestern colors and had Hopi kachina and Navajo *yei* figures adorning the walls. The Kachina Coffee Shop on the lower level of the Hi-Level lounge car also had beautiful etched-glass partitions similar to

*The Indian culture of the Southwest gave the ad designers wonderful images to incorporate into Santa Fe advertisements. Native American art became a key element in advertising and promotion. This full-page ad depicts a Pueblo Indian Flute Dancer.*

This full-page ad is a classic and uses the famous slogan and Chico to promote the Santa Fe stream-liners to the Southwest.

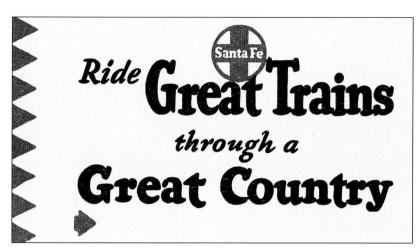

**Left**—*An ink blotter with the famous slogan printed on the face of the card.*

those in the dome lounge cars. Even the tabletops in the lounges featured Formica with Indian designs.

To further enhance the experience of the Southwest aboard Santa Fe trains, the railroad for a number of years during the 1950s hired Native American guides to ride the trains through New Mexico. These guides were primarily of Zuni and Navajo descent and they told stories and pointed out scenic highlights along the way while dressed in their native garb. Guides rode the eastbound Super Chief and the westbound El Capitan. It probably was quite a thrill for many Santa Fe passengers to get the opportunity to meet an Indian for the first time.

Another Santa Fe idea that further enabled passengers to totally experience the Southwest was the Indian Detours service, which operated in association with the Fred Harvey Co. Passengers traveling through the Southwest could detrain in Lamy, N.M., for a one-, two-, or three-day excursion to Santa Fe and various Indian and Hispanic villages throughout northern New Mexico. These side trips featured luxury touring cars and couriers, young women with college degrees and well-versed in the history of the territory, who accompanied the passengers. While on these excursions, passengers stayed at Fred Harvey hotels, then were returned to Lamy to continue their eastbound or westbound journeys. Additional Indian Detours from other Santa Fe destinations offered choices to the Petrified Forest and Grand Canyon.

In 1946, the Santa Fe created one of its most endearing advertising symbols in the form of the little Native American boy "Chico," who first appeared on the cover of Santa Fe's 1946 annual report but then went on to represent the railroad in all aspects of its advertising. The famous picture of Chico using a stick to write "Santa Fe All the Way" in the sand while a Santa Fe streamliner passes in the background decorated timetable covers and posters for many years. Over the years Chico appeared everywhere from advertisements to menus to baggage stickers. He truly became synonymous with the Santa Fe Railway. Chico even outlasted the Santa Fe streamliners, continuing to promote Santa Fe freight service after the railroad turned over its passenger service to Amtrak in 1971.

**Now**- on Super Chief and El Capitan ...

# Indian Guides across New Mexico

*Blue Wing, War Bow and Sunrise ... Pueblo Indian guides of the Indian Country.*

A real Indian, right on the train!

He's your guide to the wonders of the Indian Country.

Eastbound on the *Super Chief* and westbound on *El Capitan*, he rides with you all across his native New Mexico, enhancing your trip with tales of his people and their magic land.

A leader in his pueblo, he's educated and courteous, anxious to give you the legend and lore of his homeland.

Children love his colorful costumes and his stories about age-old tribal ceremonials and the exciting days along the old Santa Fe Trail.

For a new adventure in travel on your way to or from California ride the *Super Chief* and *El Capitan* through the romantic Indian Country on the Santa Fe.

**Take the family along!** Your travel agent or any Santa Fe passenger representative will gladly show you how much our Family Fares can reduce your travel costs. He's as near as your telephone —so why not phone him today and ask about these money-saving fares.

**Santa Fe**

*Indian guides were employed by the railroad in the 1950s to promote their native land. They rode the Super Chief and El Capitan through New Mexico and described many interesting sites along the way.*

Land of Pueblos
'roundabout Santa Fé, New Mexico

Packaged Motor tours in Indian Country planned for Santa Fe Railway patrons

Santa Fe

*Above*—An Indian guide in the Pleasure Dome on the Super Chief explains how his people live. Courtesy of the Kansas State Historical Society.

*Right*—The Santa Fe Railway offered a variety of tours to the Indian pueblos near Santa Fe, N.M. The cover of this brochure features a painting that depicts Taos Pueblo.

*Indian designs and motifs were extensively used in the decoration of the public cars on most Santa Fe streamliners. Large Hopi kachina figures in colored metal were used on the bulkheads of the Hi-Level lounge cars on El Capitan. Courtesy of the Kansas State Historical Society.*

*This circa-1950 Fred Harvey beverage list illustrates Pueblo Indian Mudhead Dancers.*

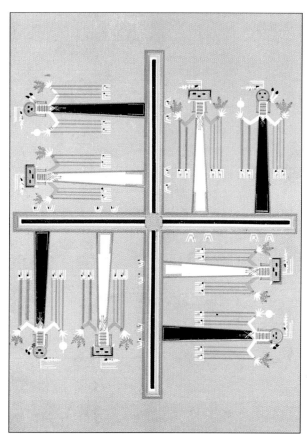

*A California Limited menu cover dated March 25, 1905, reproduces a Navajo Indian sand painting.*

*The most lavish use of Indian design and decoration was in the interior of the observation car Navajo, built for the new streamlined Super Chief in 1937. Navajo-blanket upholstery adorned the chairs and couches. Navajo yei figures framed the windows. No other Santa Fe car was ever this lavishly decorated.*

*This postcard from the late 1930s shows the interior of Cochití, the dining car on the 1937 Super Chief. The color scheme for the interior was inspired by the rich hues common to Native American art and the Southwestern landscape.*

*The Pleasure Dome lounge cars on the Super Chief were completely refurbished and redecorated in 1958 to keep them in current style. Navajo artisans were employed to create original sand paintings that adorned the bulkhead walls on either side of the entrance to the main lounge. Courtesy of the Kansas State Historical Society.*

*El Capitan received new Big Dome lounge cars in 1954. They were an instant hit with passengers and remained on El Capitan until the new Hi-Level cars were introduced in 1956. This full-page ad features one of the Indian guides who rode the train through New Mexico on a daily basis through the 1950s.*

*The Santa Fe Railway ran many ads in* National Geographic *over the years, and those that ran in the early to mid-1950s truly are unique. Indian motifs were used as design elements with great success. These ads had elegant simplicity and style that effectively captured the excitement and romance of traveling by Santa Fe streamliner through Indian country. To the right, we see a rendition from the early 1950s of a Hopi dance mask in a Super Chief ad.*

*The Super Chief was the flag-bearer of the streamlined fleet, but the Chief had been around longer and had a loyal clientele. This full-page ad illustrates the fact that the railroad still promoted the Chief in the early 1950s.*

*Above*—*Your "Grand Hotel" on rails sums up the Super Chief experience in this* National Geographic *ad from the early 1950s.*

*Right*—*The Rainbow God and Eagle Dancer motifs are used in this ad to promote the Pleasure Dome lounge car on the new 1951 Super Chief.*

THE CALIFORNIA LIMITED

*California Limited menu cover, 1915.*

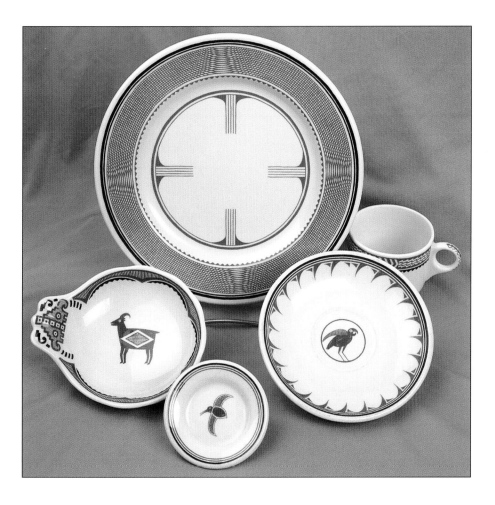

*Above*—This baggage tag from the 1937 Super Chief shows the stylized indian motif used during the 1930s and '40s.

*Left*—The famous Mimbreño-pattern china used exclusively on the Super Chief is now very collectible and rare. Ancient Mimbres Indian designs were adapted for use on this china by Mary Colter, who also designed the interiors of many of the Fred Harvey hotels such as La Fonda, La Posada and El Tovar at Grand Canyon.

*Chico graces the cover of the beverage menu used on all the streamliners through the 1960s.*

*The interior designers for the Hi-Level El Capitan used Indian motifs throughout the train to add interest and color to the cars. The Hi-Level diner shown above contained panels with kachina figures placed on dividers and bulkheads. Courtesy of the Kansas State Historical Society.*

*This* National Geographic *ad from the early 1950s promotes the Turquoise Room on the new Super Chief. A stylized Navajo* yei *figure is featured.*

*This Santa Fe promotional photograph shows the Pleasure Dome lounge car used on the Super Chief. Courtesy of the Kansas State Historical Society.*

# Film Stars Rode the Rails

By C. Fenton Richards Jr.

*Cecil B. deMille, famous film director and producer at Paramount Studios, on the platform at the Alvarado Hotel in Albuquerque, N.M., circa 1925. Photo by William Steele Dean, courtesy of the Albuquerque Museum, Negative No. 1982-128-027.*

Of all the early film studios that existed between the years of 1900 to 1913, the Biograph film company was the best. At its helm as director general was the famous D.W. Griffith, who gathered about him future film luminaries Mary Pickford, Lillian and Dorothy Gish, Blanche Sweet and Mabel Normand, the future's first great film comedienne. Mack Sennett, who started Keystone Studios, trained as actor and director of comedies under Griffith at Biograph.

On a trip back to New York from California in 1912, Biograph stopped in Albuquerque to make a couple of films. A historic two-reel Indian drama titled *A Pueblo Legend*, directed by Griffith and filmed at Isleta Pueblo and Tijeras Canyon, starred Mary Pickford, "America's Sweetheart" of the future.

Mack Sennett filmed a split-reel comedy with Mabel Normand called *The Tourist* in Albuquerque's Old Town and on the platform of the Alvarado Hotel and train depot. It marked the first time a major film company came by train to the Alvarado and Albuquerque to produce picture plays.

During the early years of filmmaking and through the 1920s and '30s, most major studios had company offices in California and New York. Paramount, for example, had film studios in Hollywood, Calif., and Astoria, Long Island, N.Y. Hence, the Santa Fe transported not only film stars between east and west, but also directors, producers and the money men behind the scenes. One of the most important stops was in Albuquerque at the Alvarado, where the film folk could eat, buy Native American souvenirs and be photographed by the locals with their Kodaks. Star-struck William Steele Dean was among those who regularly photographed celebrities on the Alvarado platform throughout the 1920s. His photo collection is on display at the Albuquerque Museum, complete with some of his best pictures of the most famous and important film figures of the 1920s.

In 1945, MGM released a major Technicolor musical entitled *The Harvey Girls*, starring Judy Garland and made in cooperation with and dedicated to the Fred Harvey Co. It told the story of a group of young women exported to the Southwest by the Fred Harvey Co. on the Atchison, Topeka & Santa Fe Railway to be hostesses at a Harvey House. This film made a hit out of the song written by Johnny Mercer and Harry Warren, "On the Atchison, Topeka & Santa Fe." So exuberant was this song extolling the virtues of the railway company that it even won an Academy Award for Mercer and Warren for Song of the Year. Many versions of the song were recorded and New Mexico is mentioned in most of them. When Johnny Mercer recorded his version of lyrics, he even mentions Albuquerque on the route the train takes cross-country.

The Santa Fe's swansong as movie star was also one for silent-film star Gloria Swanson, one of the biggest names from the halcyon days when silents ruled. In the film *Three for Bedroom C*, Swanson portrayed a film star hiding out with her daughter on the Santa Fe Super Chief. But the train proved to be the real star, for most of the action in the film took place aboard the train. Though unique for being only one of a handful of films that takes place entirely within a train and its different cars, this film did naught to revitalize Swanson's waning career or that of the Super Chief. By the mid-1950s travel by air and car became the dominate modes of transportation. The rapidity of air travel and the freedom afforded by a car on the road led to the demise of the train as the preferred mode of travel for film stars—and the Super Chief as the star of trains.

**Above**—*The courtyard of the Alvarado Hotel in Albuquerque, circa 1920. Photo by William Steele Dean, courtesy of the Albuquerque Museum, Negative No. 1982-128-240.*

**Left**—*Famed boxer Jack Dempsey and his actress-wife Estelle Taylor purchase curios from a vendor at the Fred Harvey Indian Building at the Alvarado Hotel in Albquerque, circa 1925. Photo by William Steele Dean, courtesy of the Albuquerque Museum, Negative No. 1982-128-072.*

*Famous Paramount Studios actress Lois Wilson, star of the first epic Western made in 1923,* The Covered Wagon, *poses in front of the Fred Harvey Indian Building at the Alvarado Hotel in Albuquerque. Photo by William Steele Dean, courtesy of the Albuquerque Museum, Negative No. 1982-128-111.*

*The talented tots of producer Hal Roach's* Our Gang *comedies, on a train tour in the late 1920s. From left to right, Mary Ann Jackson, Jean Darling, Harry Spear, "Farina" Allen Hoskins and Joe Cobb. Photo by William Steele Dean, courtesy of the Albuquerque Museum, Negative No. 1982-128-082.*

*Leading Latin Lothario of the silent screen, Rudolph Valentino, walks his dog on the platform of the Albuquerque Depot, circa 1924. Photo by William Steele Dean, courtesy of the Albuquerque Museum, Negative No. 1982-128-088.*

*Albuquerque's own Don Alvarado, silent-film leading man in D. W. Griffith's pictures* Drums of Love *and* The Battle of the Sexes, *circa 1928. Photo by William Steele Dean, courtesy of the Albuquerque Museum, Negative No. 1982-128-020.*

*Rin-Tin-Tin, major Warner Brothers star and money-maker of the 1920s, is seen here with his mate and their offspring. "Rinty" is on the left with his trainer, circa 1928. Photo by William Steele Dean, courtesy of the Albuquerque Museum, Negative No. 1982-128-160.*

*Dorothy Gish, famous sister of Lillian Gish, was to comedy in films what Lillian was to drama. She wears a stylish ensemble on the platform at the Albuquerque Station, circa 1924. Photo by William Steele Dean, courtesy of the Albuquerque Museum, Negative No. 1982-128-041.*

*Above*—A lovely portrait of confetti-covered Mary Pickford, "America's Sweetheart," the most famous actress of the silent era, circa 1926. Photo by William Steele Dean, courtesy of the Albuquerque Museum, Negative No. 1982-128-038.

*Right*—Harold Lloyd, thrill-comedian sans horn-rimmed glasses, in front of a Santa Fe train in Albuquerque, circa 1924. Photo by William Steele Dean, courtesy of the Albuquerque Museum, Negative No. 1982-128-013.

*Above*—Hollywood's royal couple, Douglas Fairbanks Sr. and wife Mary Pickford, stop in Albuquerque while traveling cross-country. They are greeted by Albuquerque Mayor Clyde Tingley on the right, circa 1924. Photo by William Steele Dean, courtesy of the Albuquerque Museum, Negative No. 1982-128-060.

*Right*—Sheet music from the MGM picture The Harvey Girls. This song won an Academy Award for Song of the Year. Courtesy of the Rosalie Purvis Collection.

*Queen of the MGM lot for more than a decade, Norma Shearer is seen here in front of the Fred Harvey Indian Building in Albuquerque, circa 1926, before her marriage to boy-genius producer Irving Thalberg. Photo by William Steele Dean, courtesy of the Albuquerque Museum, Negative No. 1982-128-023.*

*Samuel Goldwyn, famous film producer and starmaker, with his wife on the platform in front of the Alvarado Hotel in Albuquerque, circa 1927. Photo by William Steele Dean, courtesy of the Albuquerque Museum, Negative No. 1982-128-165.*

# The Santa Fe Railway Art Collection

Caravan—Santa Fe Trail
*Private Collection*

**W**illiam Haskell Simpson became the Santa Fe's general advertising agent in 1900 and immediately embarked on a campaign to change the company's image and aggressively promote tourism to the Southwest. He proved to be a genius in this effort.

Simpson initially offered artists from the East trips to the Grand Canyon in exchange for the use of their paintings in Santa Fe advertising. Soon, however, Simpson and the railroad's management decided it best to actually purchase the paintings and avoid possible problems with reproduction rights.

The first painting Simpson purchased in 1903 illustrated the San Francisco Peaks in northern Arizona, painted by Bertha Menzler Dressler. By 1907 Simpson had acquired an additional 108 paintings. The majority of the paintings depicted Southwestern landscapes or were portraits of Native Americans living in New Mexico and Arizona. As time went on, Simpson also commissioned paintings of specific subjects he wanted included in the railroad's collection. In the process the Santa Fe Railway became a prominent patron of Taos and Santa Fe artists. Simpson and the railroad did much to financially support the Taos and Santa Fe art colonies, and the acquired paintings did much to promote tourism to the Southwest on Santa Fe trains.

While reproductions of these paintings illustrated all types of advertising, perhaps the most famous venue was the annual Santa Fe calendars, hundreds of thousands of which were sent to schools and businesses all over the country. The first use of a railroad painting on a calendar was in 1907, another Simpson idea. The Santa Fe calendar tradition continued long after Simpson's death and, in fact, lasted until 1993. Today, collectors of railroad memorabilia and Southwestern art pay high prices for old Santa Fe calendar prints.

After World War II the railroad printed reproductions of its paintings on the covers of menus used in the dining cars of all the streamliners. These full-color menus included a description of the painting and the artist on the back.

Even after Simpson's death in 1933, the railroad continued his legacy of purchasing original paintings. Today, the Santa Fe's collection exceeds 600 paintings and includes works by such noted artists as Thomas Moran, Louis Akin, E. Irving Couse, Gerald Cassidy, Ernest Blumenschein, Bert Geer Phillips, Bettina Steinke and many others. The collection is one of the largest of Southwestern art in existence and also one of the finest. The railroad still owns the collection and the paintings now hang in the railroad's corporate offices in Fort Worth, Texas, and other offices around the system. In 1966, the collection became available for exhibition and has toured nationwide from the National Archives in Washington, D.C., to the New Mexico Museum of Fine Arts in Santa Fe, N.M.

Navajo Ponies *by Gerard C. Delano*
*Private Collection*

Kachina Doll *by E. Irving Couse*
*Private Collection*

Monument Valley—Arizona *by Gerard C. Delano*
*Courtesy of the Burlington Northern and Santa Fe Railway Company*

Turquoise Bead Maker *by E. Irving Couse*
*Courtesy of the Burlington Northern and Santa Fe Railway Company*

Taos Pueblo *by Frederic Mizen*
*Private Collection*

Tesuque Valley *by Theodore Van Soelen*
*Courtesy of the Burlington Northern and Santa Fe Railway Company*

Ranchos de Taos *by Ernest Blumenschein*
*Private Collection*

The Blanket Weaver *by E. Irving Couse*
*Private Collection*

Monument Valley *by Charles Waldo Love*
*Courtesy of the Burlington Northern and Santa Fe Railway Company*

Navajo Shepherdess *by Gerard C. Delano*
*Courtesy of the Burlington Northern and Santa Fe Railway Company*

Pueblo Market *by John Hauser*
*Private Collection*

Street Scene in Taos, New Mexico *by Leonard Reedy*
*Courtesy of the Burlington Northern and Santa Fe Railway Company*

# Down By the Depot

*The depot in Portales, N.M. Hand-tinted photograph by C. Fenton Richards Jr.*

As the Santa Fe laid tracks across New Mexico, it constructed wood-frame depots in the communities along its route. These stations handled the town's passenger and freight business and functioned as the railroad's operating headquarters in each community. In the early years of the 20th century, many of these frame depots in the larger towns were replaced by much more substantial structures built of brick, concrete and stucco. In New Mexico, these new larger stations were built in such towns as Ratón, Las Vegas, Santa Fe, Albuquerque, Clovis, Las Cruces and Gallup. All of these stations were built in the Southwestern Pueblo or Mission style of architecture. The brown stucco used on the exteriors of the buildings made them appear as if they were constructed of adobe similar to the Indian pueblos of the area.

Many of these stations were also built with Fred Harvey hotels and restaurants, adjacent to or actually connected, in Las Vegas, Lamy, Clovis, Gallup and Albuquerque. With the railroad station, hotel and restaurant located together, these complexes soon became the social gathering places of their communities and remained so until after World War II, when the automobile began to drastically alter the social fabric of American cities.

Of all the Santa Fe station and Fred Harvey hotel/restaurant complexes, the Alvarado Hotel in Albuquerque was without a doubt the largest and most famous. Besides its 118 guest rooms, the Alvarado also contained a formal dining room, coffee shop, ballroom, cocktail lounge, beauty and barber shops, and newsstand.

With its vine-covered walkways and gardens with fountains, the Alvarado was an oasis in downtown Albuquerque. Its world-famous Fred Harvey Indian Building displayed a large collection of museum-quality Indian and Mexican handicrafts and sold jewelry, pottery, baskets and rugs to tourists. It was a time-honored tradition for fascinated Santa Fe passengers to step off their train in Albuquerque during its service stop and visit the Fred Harvey Indian Building at the Alvarado Hotel.

Unfortunately, most of the Fred Harvey hotels have been gone for many years, including the Alvarado, which closed in 1969 and was demolished in 1970. The city of Las Vegas, N.M., however, still has two standing Harvey hotels, the Castañeda and the Montezuma Castle, although both have been closed for many years. Former Harvey houses La Fonda in Santa Fe, N.M., La Posada in Winslow, Ariz., and El Tovar and the Bright Angel Lodge at Grand Canyon are still open in 2001. Amazingly, most of the major Santa Fe depots built in New Mexico nearly a century ago still remain, and some of them are still used today by Amtrak passenger trains. Tragically, the Albuquerque depot burned to the ground in January 1993.

*The depot in Ratón, N.M. Hand-tinted photograph by C. Fenton Richards Jr.*

*The depot in Lamy, N.M. Hand-tinted photograph by C. Fenton Richards Jr.*

*The depot in Fort Sumner, N.M. Hand-tinted photograph by C. Fenton Richards Jr.*

*The depot at Belén, N.M. Hand-tinted photograph by C. Fenton Richards Jr.*

*The depot in Las Vegas, N.M. Hand-tinted photograph by C. Fenton Richards Jr.*

*The restored depot in Gallup, N.M. Hand-tinted photograph by C. Fenton Richards Jr.*

*The depot in Mountainair, N.M. Hand-tinted photograph by C. Fenton Richards Jr.*

*The depot in Vaughn, N.M. Hand-tinted photograph by C. Fenton Richards Jr.*

*The depot in Albuquerque, N.M., is seen in this 1930s postcard before the tower was modified.*

*The fountain and courtyard of the Alvarado Hotel in Albuquerque.*

*The wood-frame depot in Magdalena, N.M. Hand-tinted photograph by C. Fenton Richards Jr.*

*The depot in Clovis, N.M. Hand-tinted photograph by C. Fenton Richards Jr.*

*The Montezuma Castle, initially built in the late 1880s by the Santa Fe Railway as a spa and resort hotel, near Las Vegas, N.M. Hand-tinted Van Dyke photograph by C. Fenton Richards Jr.*

*The firehouse at the train yard in Albuquerque. Hand-tinted photograph by C. Fenton Richards Jr.*

*The Fred Harvey Castañeda Hotel in Las Vegas. Hand-tinted photograph by C. Fenton Richards Jr.*

*The depot in Melrose, N.M. Hand-tinted photograph by C. Fenton Richards Jr.*

*The depot in Albuquerque as it appeared in 1982. Tragically, the depot burned to the ground in January 1993. Photograph by C. Fenton Richards Jr.*

# Off to the Happy Hunting Grounds

*off-season*

# Bargain Fares

## are back!

**Santa Fe**

Come travel at special low round trip fares from September 15, 1966 to May 15, 1967

*Cover of a pamphlet promoting bargain fares in the late 1960s.*

After World War II the Santa Fe Railway was poised to provide first-rate train service to millions of Americans who had the time and money to explore their country. Between 1945 and the mid-1950s, Santa Fe invested millions of dollars on new passenger cars and diesel locomotives to virtually replace its entire fleet of passenger trains. It also began an intense advertising campaign to attract travelers to these new trains. For a while the passenger business boomed, and it's arguable that the decade following the end of the war actually was the heyday of the American streamliner.

But a storm of change in other areas of transportation also occurred during this time. Americans started buying new automobiles at a feverish pace and the country went on a highway-building frenzy. People preferred the freedom that the automobile gave them to go wherever and whenever they wanted. Also during this period commercial-airline travel became more affordable and popular, so that by the mid-1950s fewer people traveled by train. Many railroads, discouraged by dwindling number of train travelers as of the late 1950s, began to dismantle their passenger services. The Santa Fe, instead, trimmed its money-losing services but still found ways to cut expenses while operating its premier trains in a top-notch manner. It continued to advertise its trains and offered money-saving fares to attract passengers.

These efforts worked for a while, but in the fall of 1967 the death knell basically sounded for the privately owned passenger train in America. The U.S. Postal Service notified the nation's railroads that it was terminating its railway post office contracts and that all first-class mail would be sent by air from then on. This delivered a great blow to passenger service as the revenues generated from the mail contracts contributed a substantial amount of income to passenger-train operations. Without this capital it became extremely difficult to operate passenger trains at a profit. Santa Fe's management faced the agonizing task of deciding whether to continue operating some of its more popular passenger trains. By the summer of 1968, the railroad eliminated almost all of its less-popular, money-losing trains. In fact, the only trains still operating were the Super Chief, El Capitan, San Francisco Chief, Texas Chief, trains between Los Angeles and San Diego, and a three-car Chicago to Los Angeles local train, a remnant of the once famous Grand Canyon Limited. The most noteworthy train terminated in 1968 was the famed Chief, which had run daily since 1926.

*The round-end observation car on the Chief provided an inviting spot to relax and view the passing scenery. Courtesy of the Kansas State Historical Society.*

*The eastbound Chief approaches the west portal of Ratón Tunnel at Lynn, N.M., just weeks before it was discontinued. Photograph by Ernest Robart.*

*The last Santa Fe train #17, the Super Chief-El Capitan, awaits departure from Albuquerque, N.M., on May 1, 1971. Photograph by Ernest Robart.*

*The last run of Santa Fe train #23, the Grand Canyon, arrives in Albuquerque on May 1, 1971. Photograph by Ernest Robart.*

The trains that the Santa Fe kept in service continued to operate in the grand Santa Fe tradition. Some amenities were eliminated, but generally the trains were still first-rate. By the late 1960s, however, passenger-train losses became intolerable. Thus in 1971 the U.S. government created Amtrak to take over and operate the remaining passenger trains in the country. Railroads were not required to join Amtrak, and the Santa Fe Railway management thought long and hard before they finally decided to turn their famous streamliners over to the new service. On May 1, 1971, the Santa Fe Railway dropped the passenger business as Amtrak began operating the nation's passenger trains.

For several years, Amtrak continued to operate the Super Chief, El Capitan and Texas Chief with the same care as the Santa Fe, using all of the same equipment with former Santa Fe employees. Little by little, however, Amtrak began downgrading the service on these trains, and when the first-class dining car was eliminated on the Super Chief, the railroad informed Amtrak that they held copyright to the name "Chief" and that the name could no longer be used. Thus the Super Chief name quietly slipped into oblivion after almost 40 years. On December 31, 1996, the Atchison, Topeka and Santa Fe Railway merged with the Burlington Northern Railroad to become the Burlington Northern and Santa Fe Railway. After 136 years, the Atchison, Topeka and Santa Fe Railway, too, passed into the history annals.

*Santa Fe train #17, the westbound Super Chief-El Capitan, passes the Bernalillo, N.M., station on March 15, 1971. Photograph by Ernest Robart.*

*Santa Fe train #2, the San Francisco Chief eastbound, approaches Dalies, N.M., on February 28, 1971. Photograph by Ernest Robart.*

*Amtrak train #3, the Super Chief-El Capitan westbound, just north of Ratón, N.M., descends Ratón Pass on January 17, 1972. Photograph by Ernest Robart.*

*Amtrak train #3, the Super Chief-El Capitan, in Belén, N.M., westbound on a reroute because of a freight train derailment at Nueve Siding near San Felipe Pueblo on September 15, 1972. Photograph by Ernest Robart.*

*Santa Fe train #17 pauses in Belén at 10:20 p.m. on a rerouting due to the closing of the main line in western Kansas because of drifting snow on February 23, 1971. Photograph by Ernest Robart.*

*Amtrak train #3, the Super Chief-El Capitan, speeds through Wagon Mound, N.M., at 80 mph, running about four hours late on January 14, 1973. Photograph by Ernest Robart.*

*Amtrak train #3, the Super Chief-El Capitan, arrives in Albuquerque while en route to Los Angeles on May 14, 1972. Photograph by Ernest Robart.*

*The first Amtrak train #17, the Super Chief-El Capitan, arrives in Albuquerque on May 2, 1971. Photograph by Ernest Robart.*

# Epilogue

I f you ever find yourself along old Route 66 in western New Mexico with the Red Cliffs to the north, pull off the road and walk over to the railroad tracks. The sound you hear is probably the wind blowing through the trees atop the Continental Divide, but it also might be the spirit of the westbound Super Chief chasing the setting sun. The spirits of the Santa Fe Railway and its famous streamliners still roam the American Southwest.

*Courtesy of the Kansas State Historical Society.*

# Bibliography

*The Harvey Girls*, Lesley Poling-Kemps, Paragon House, 1989

*History of the Atchison, Topeka and Santa Fe Railway*, Keith L. Bryant Jr., University of Nebraska Press, 1974

*Santa Fe Depots: The Western Lines*, Robert E. Pounds, Kachina Press, 1984

*Santa Fe Streamliners*, Karl Zimmermann, Quadrant Press, 1987

*Santa Fe: The Railroad That Built an Empire*, James Marshall, Random House, 1945

*Trademarks of the Santa Fe Railway*, Richard W. Pelouze, Santa Fe Railway Historical and Modeling Society, 1997

*Twilight of the Great Trains*, Fred W. Frailey, Kalmbach, 1998

*Visions and Visionaries: The Art and Artists of the Santa Fe Railway*, Sandra D'Emilio and Suzan Campbell, Gibbs Smith, 1991

# The Authors

**Robert Strein** was 2 years old when his family moved to New Mexico in 1949, and he has lived there ever since. He has been a fan of the Santa Fe Railway for as long as he can remember. During the summers of 1969 and 1970, while attending the University of New Mexico in Albuquerque, he worked for the Santa Fe Railway Dining Car Department in Chicago as a waiter in the Kachina Coffee Shop on the lower level of El Capitan's Hi-Level lounge car, running between Chicago and Los Angeles. After graduating from college, Strein embarked on a 26-year career with the State of New Mexico. He retired several years ago and still lives in New Mexico's capital, Santa Fe.

**John Vaughan** is a native New Mexican born and raised in Hobbs, N.M. He is an avid collector of Santa Fe Railway memorabilia. After graduating from the University of Denver, he embarked on a career as a graphic designer in El Paso, Texas, and Albuquerque. He commutes daily (by automobile) from his home in Albuquerque to Santa Fe, where he is the art director for *New Mexico Magazine*.

**C. Fenton Richards Jr.** has always been a child of the Southwest, born in Phoeniz, Ariz., in 1955. At the tender age of 4, his air-traffic-controller father moved the family to Stanley, N.M., where future Governor and First Lady Bruce and Alice King were the landlords of the house his family rented. From 1960 to 1965, Richard's family lived in Zuni, N.M., where the vistas and changing colors on the mesas influenced his vision and imagination's palette. An Albuquerque resident since 1965, Richards studied psychology and sociology at the University of New Mexico, earning a degree in psychology. Influenced by an artist friend in 1980, Richards took up photography and studied at UNM. His work is heavily influenced by the pictorialist movement and photographers from the turn of the last century.